OXFORD
UNIVERSITY PRESS

What's Inside Me?

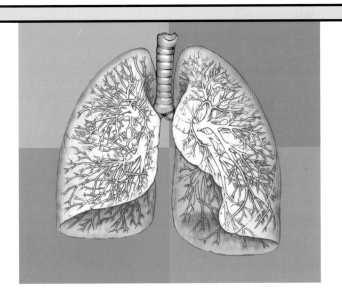

Carnegie Primary
School

Diana Noonan

Contents

Introduction

On the outside, everyone looks different. Some people have dark hair. Some people have fair hair. Some people are tall. Some people are short.

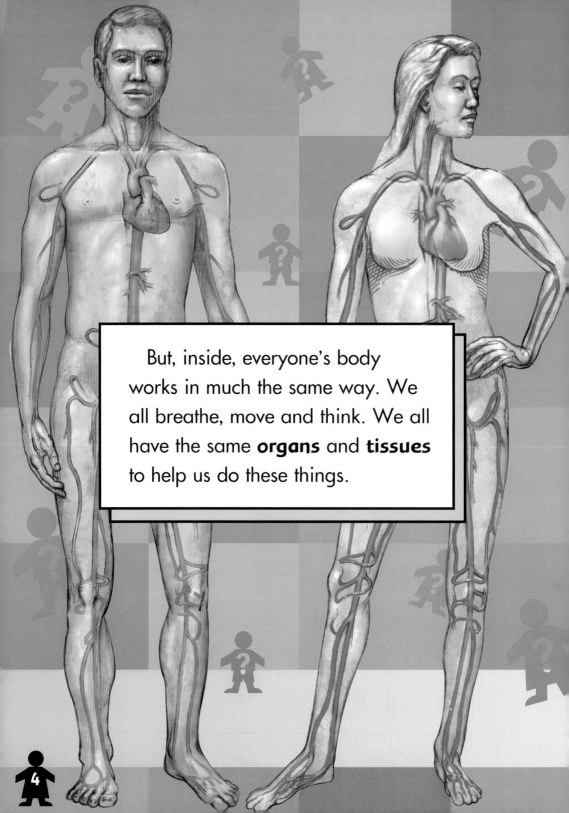

But, inside, everyone's body works in much the same way. We all breathe, move and think. We all have the same **organs** and **tissues** to help us do these things.

Lungs

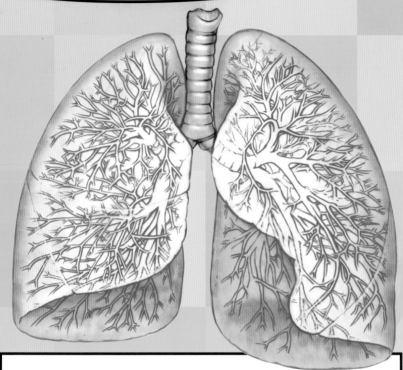

Inside your chest are two stretchy lungs that help you breathe. They stretch out when you breathe in. They shrink back when you breathe out.

Did you know...
that your right lung is bigger than your left lung?

When you breathe in, your lungs collect **oxygen** gas from the air. When you breathe out, they push gas out of your body. The gas is called **carbon dioxide**.

Air pollution from a factory

Cigarette smoke

Breathing cigarette smoke can damage your lungs. Air pollution can also harm your lungs.

Blood

Arteries

Carry blood away from your heart to your body

Veins

Carry blood from your body back to your heart

Blood carries the **oxygen** your body needs. Your blood travels all around your body in tubes of different sizes.

The tubes that carry blood and **oxygen** are called arteries. The tubes that carry blood and **carbon dioxide** are called veins.

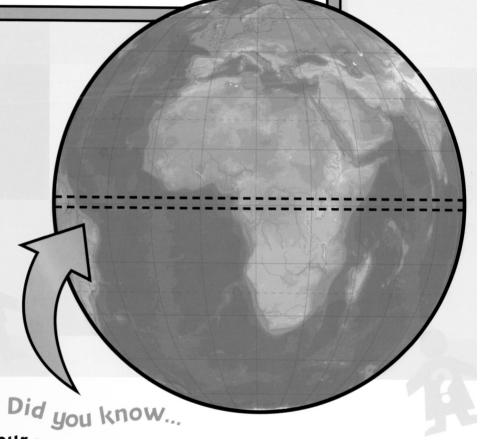

Did you know...
your veins and arteries are so long they would go around the world twice?

Heart

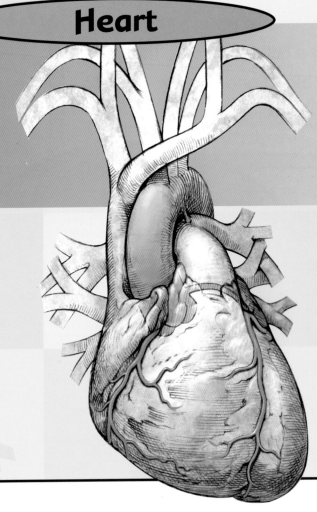

Your heart is a muscle. It forces blood around your body. It makes a beating sound as it squeezes in tightly, then swells back out to its normal size. This squeezing and swelling pulls and pushes blood through the veins and arteries.

Did you know...
**that your heart is strong enough
to squirt blood easily from
one side of the classroom to the other?**

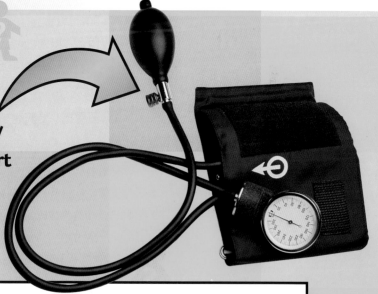

This machine
measures how
well your heart
is pushing the
blood around
your body.

It takes about one minute for blood
to travel around your body and back
to your heart.

An adult's heart beats between 60
and 70 times a minute. A child's heart
beats faster than an adult's.

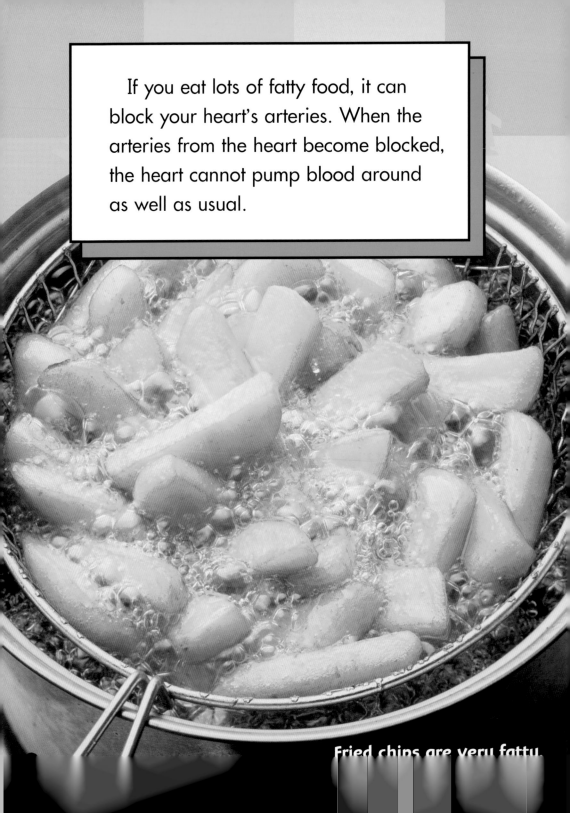

If you eat lots of fatty food, it can block your heart's arteries. When the arteries from the heart become blocked, the heart cannot pump blood around as well as usual.

Fried chips are very fatty.

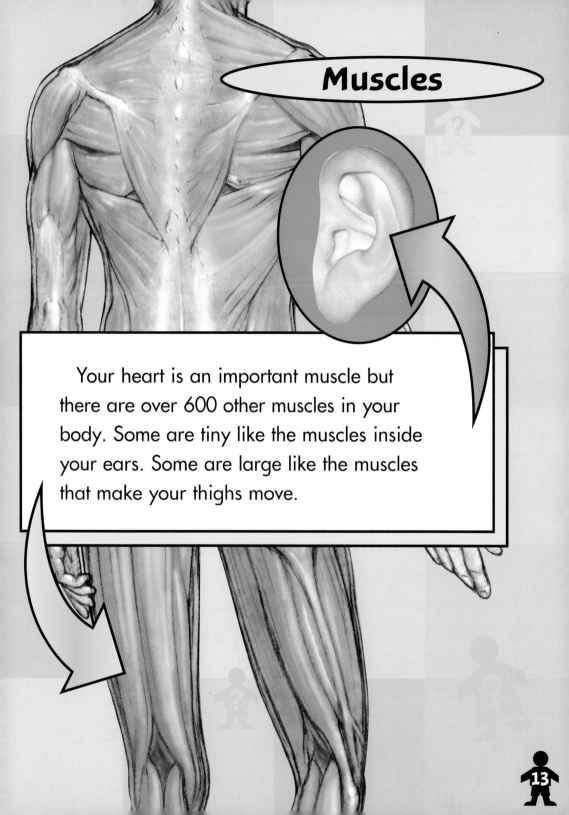

Muscles

Your heart is an important muscle but there are over 600 other muscles in your body. Some are tiny like the muscles inside your ears. Some are large like the muscles that make your thighs move.

You need fuel for your muscles to be able to ride a bike.

Muscles need **oxygen** and sugar to help them work well. Blood carries this **fuel** to the muscles. The more you exercise, the more fuel your muscles need. That is why your heart beats faster when you exercise. It is carrying more blood to your muscles.

Did you know...
that the tongue is the strongest muscle
in the body for its size?

Some muscles, like your heart, move even when you are asleep. Other muscles, such as arm muscles, move only when you want to make them work.

Did you know...

that you exercise at least 17 muscles when you smile?

Brain

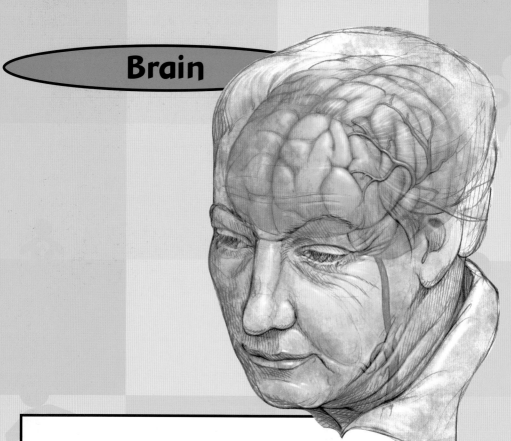

Your brain is soft and jelly-like and contains lots of cells. It is protected by your hard skull. An adult's brain weighs about 1.4 kg.

Did you know...

that the brain gets lighter as you get older because cells die and are not replaced?

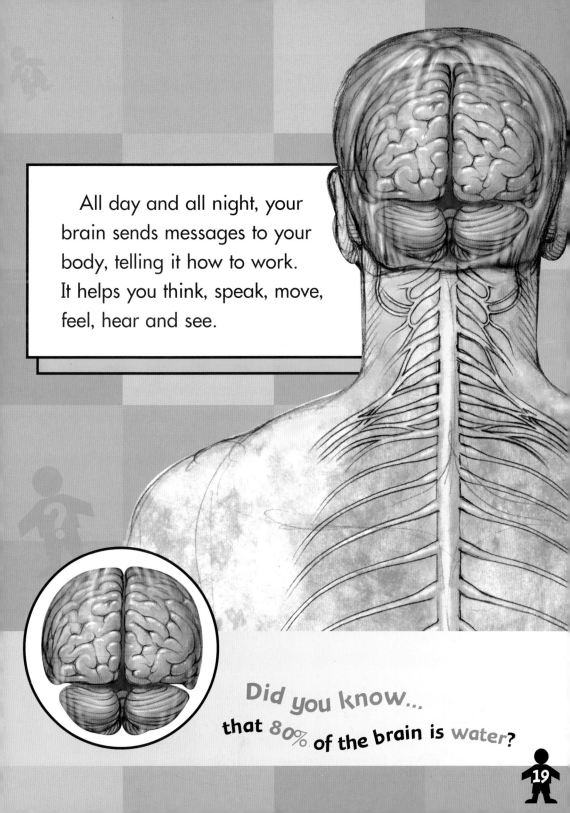

All day and all night, your brain sends messages to your body, telling it how to work. It helps you think, speak, move, feel, hear and see.

Did you know... that 80% of the brain is water?

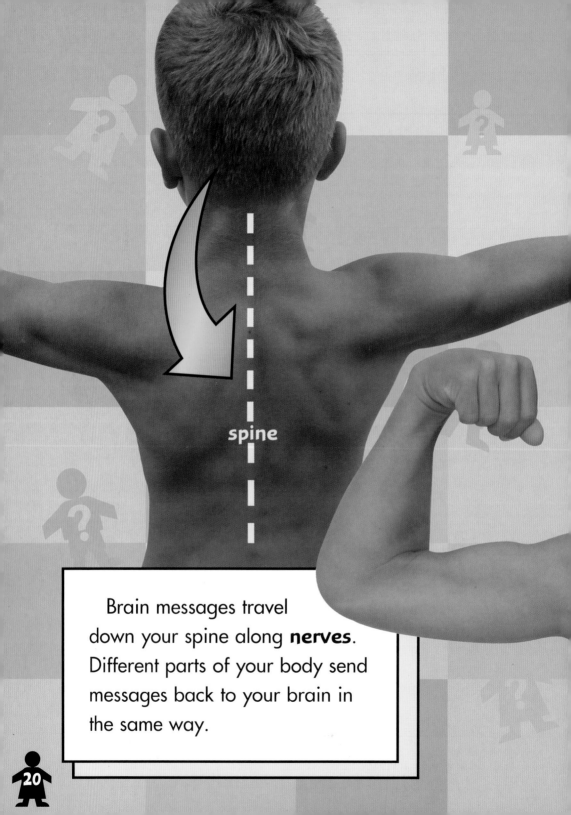

spine

Brain messages travel down your spine along **nerves**. Different parts of your body send messages back to your brain in the same way.

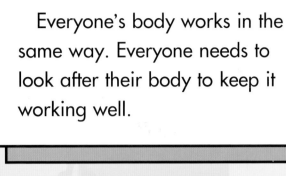

Everyone's body works in the same way. Everyone needs to look after their body to keep it working well.

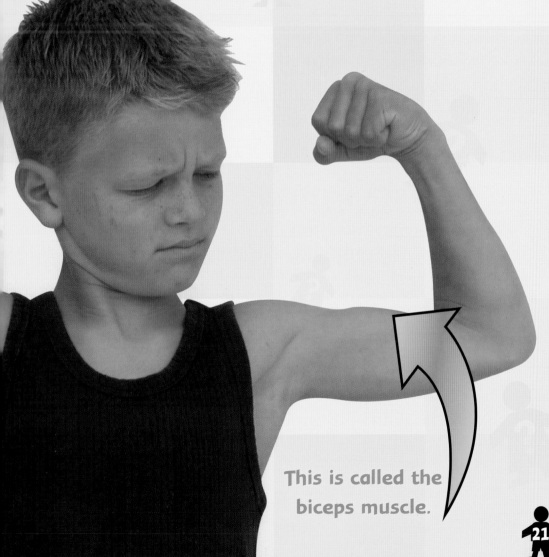

This is called the biceps muscle.

Take Care of Your Body

Exercise
- Ride your bike or your skateboard.
- Go to a dance class.
- Walk with your family or friends.
- Play at the park.

Rest
- Go to bed early whenever you can.
- Do not have too many late nights.

Eat Well
- Eat plenty of fresh fruit and vegetables.
- Don't eat sweets and junk food very often.

Glossary

carbon dioxide – A gas that people make by breathing. It has no colour or smell.

fuel – Food and oxygen that give the body the energy it needs to work properly.

nerves – Parts of the body that send messages to the brain.

organs – Parts of the body that each have their own special job.

oxygen – The gas we need to breathe. It has no colour or smell.

tissues – The materials from which humans are made.

Index